PIANO | VOCAL | GUITAR

LAUREN DAIGLE
LOOK UP CHILD

ISBN 978-1-5400-3781-7

Visit Hal Leonard Online at
www.halleonard.com

Contact Us:
Hal Leonard
7777 West Bluemound Road
Milwaukee, WI 53213
Email: info@halleonard.com

In Europe contact:
Hal Leonard Europe Limited
42 Wigmore Street
Marylebone, London, W1U 2RN
Email: info@halleonardeurope.com

In Australia contact:
Hal Leonard Australia Pty. Ltd.
4 Lentara Court
Cheltenham, Victoria, 3192 Australia
Email: info@halleonard.com.au

CONTENTS

STILL ROLLING STONES

Words and Music by LAUREN DAIGLE,
PAUL DUNCAN, JASON INGRAM
and PAUL MABURY

9

THIS GIRL

Words and Music by LAUREN DAIGLE,
PAUL DUNCAN, JASON INGRAM
and PAUL MABURY

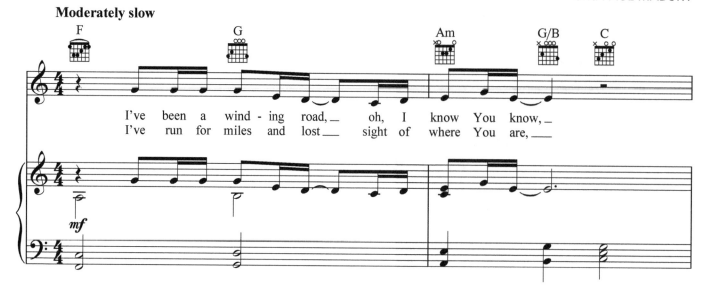

RESCUE

Words and Music by LAUREN DAIGLE,
JASON INGRAM and PAUL MABURY

* Recorded a half step lower.

YOUR WINGS

Words and Music by LAUREN DAIGLE,
JASON INGRAM, PAUL MABURY
and LAUREN STRAHM

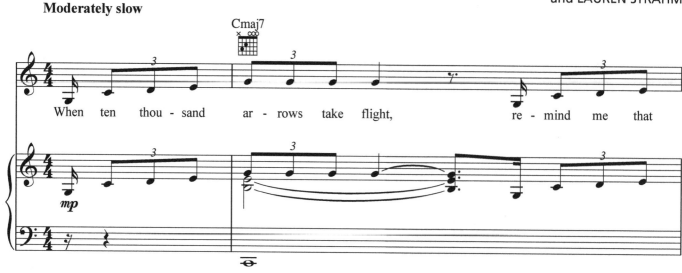

When ten thou-sand ar-rows take flight, re-mind me that

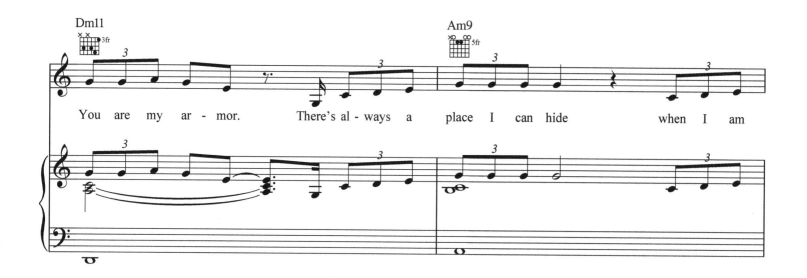

You are my ar-mor. There's al-ways a place I can hide when I am

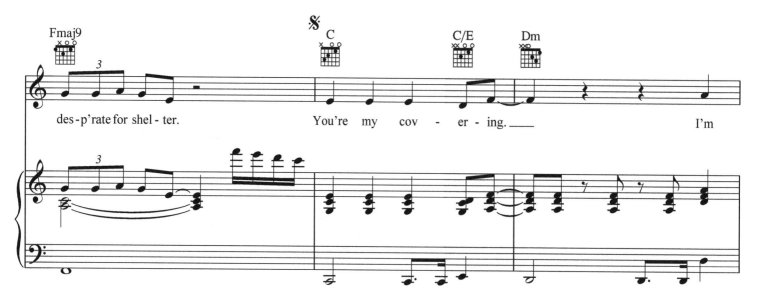

des-p'rate for shel-ter. You're my cov-er-ing. I'm

EVERYTHING

Words and Music by LAUREN DAIGLE,
JASON INGRAM and PAUL MABURY

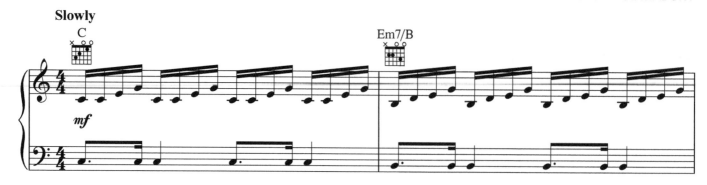

E- ven the spar-

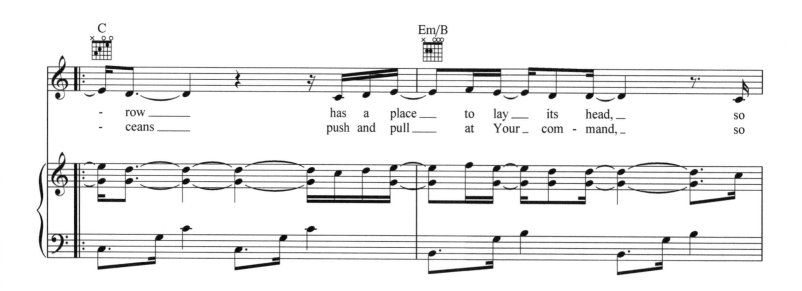

- row _____ has a place _____ to lay _____ its head, _____ so

- ceans _____ push and pull _____ at Your _ com - mand, _ so

YOU SAY

Words and Music by LAUREN DAIGLE,
JASON INGRAM and PAUL MABURY

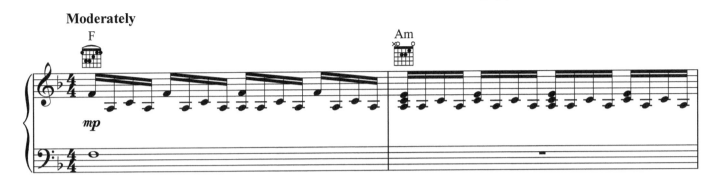

I keep fight-ing voic-es in my mind that say I'm not e - nough,

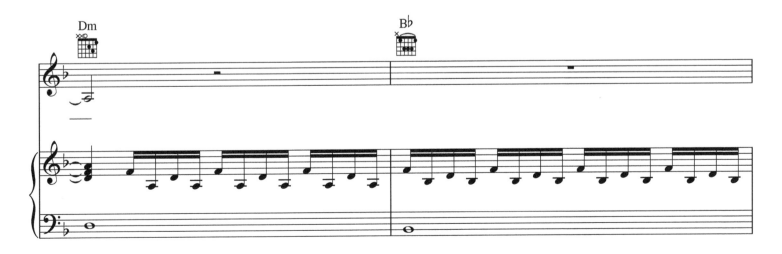

Oh, I be - lieve. ___ Yes, I be - lieve ___

___ what You say ___ of me. ___ I be - lieve. ___

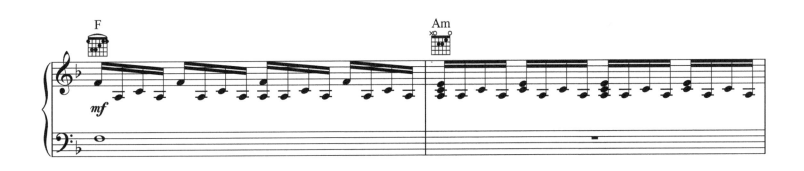

LOOK UP CHILD

Words and Music by LAUREN DAIGLE,
JASON INGRAM and PAUL MABURY

LOSING MY RELIGION

Words and Music by LAUREN DAIGLE,
JASON INGRAM and PAUL MABURY

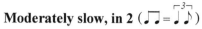

Moderately slow, in 2

I've been an ac - tor on ___ a stage, ___
No more per-form - ing out ___ of fear. ___
Light ___ a match ___ and watch ___ it burn. ___

play - ing the role ___ I have ___ to play. ___
I'm try - ing to keep ___ my con - science clear. ___
To Your ___ heart ___ I will ___ re - turn. ___

D.S. al Coda

LOVE LIKE THIS

Words and Music by LAUREN DAIGLE,
JASON INGRAM and PAUL MABURY

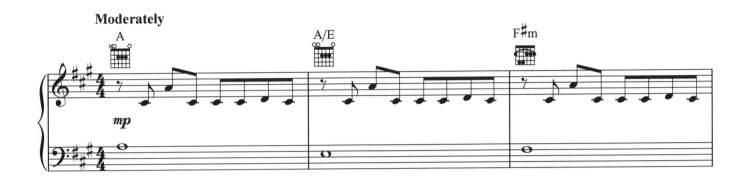

When I ___ am a waste - land, ___
When I ___ am a long ___ night, ___
Your voice ___ like a whis - per, ___

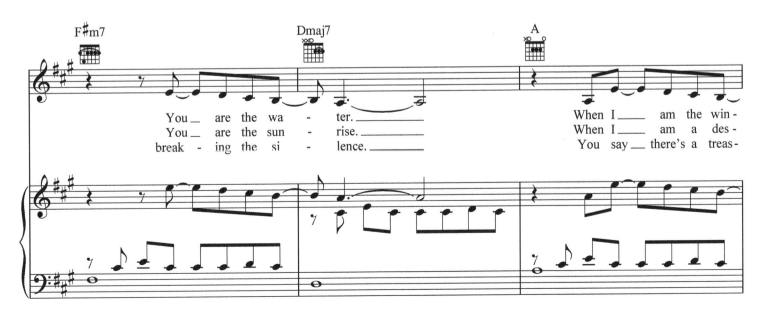

You ___ are the wa - ter. ___
You ___ are the sun - rise. ___
break - ing the si - lence. ___

When I ___ am the win -
When I ___ am a des -
You say ___ there's a treas -

REMEMBER

Words and Music by LAUREN DAIGLE,
CHRIS TOMLIN, JASON INGRAM
and PAUL MABURY

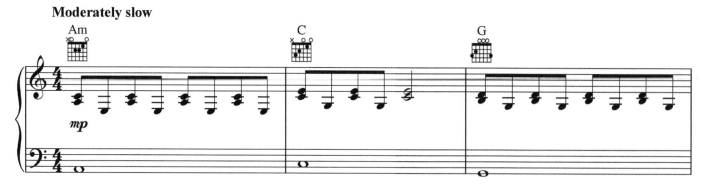

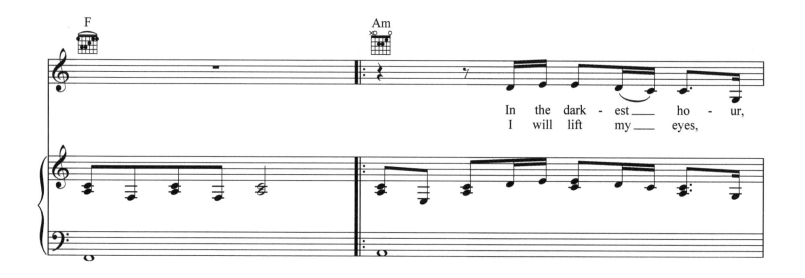

In the dark - est ___ ho - ur,
I will lift my ___ eyes,

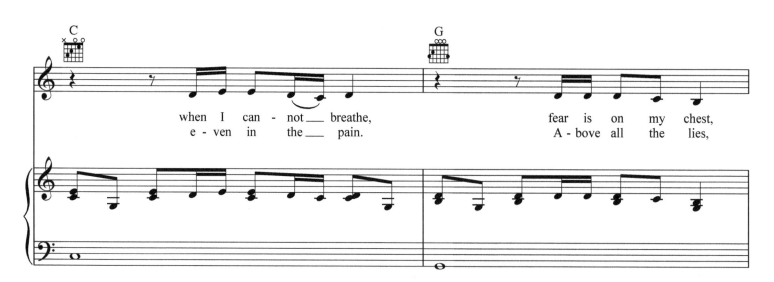

when I can - not ___ breathe,
e - ven in the ___ pain.

fear is on my chest,
A - bove all the lies,

REBEL HEART

Words and Music by LAUREN DAIGLE,
PAUL DUNCAN and PAUL MABURY

TURN YOUR EYES UPON JESUS

Words and Music by LAUREN DAIGLE,
DWAN HILL and PAUL MABURY

Moderately slow, relaxed feel

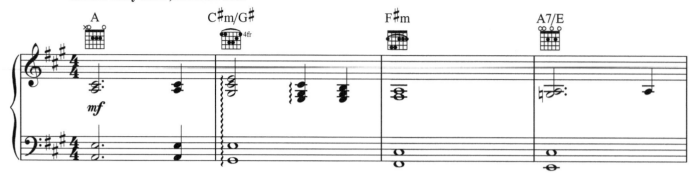

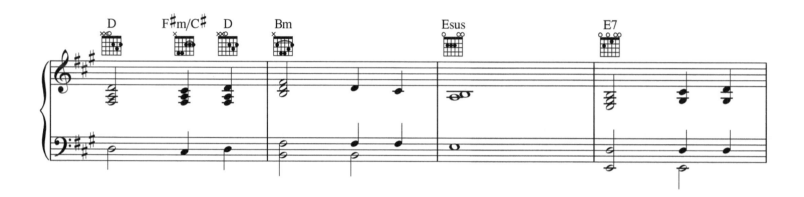

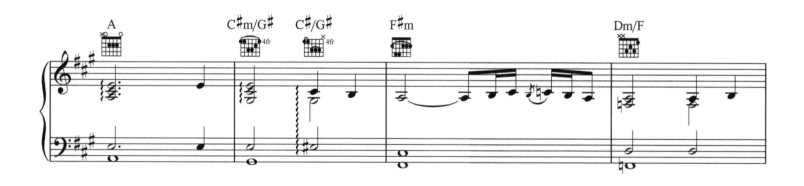

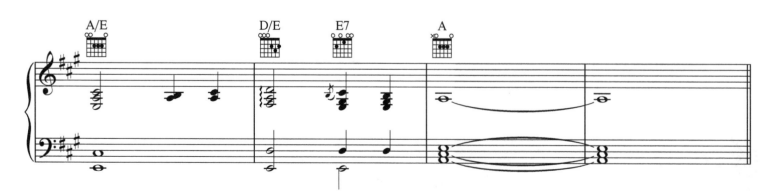

INEVITABLE

Words and Music by LAUREN DAIGLE,
PAUL DUNCAN and PAUL MABURY

Slowly

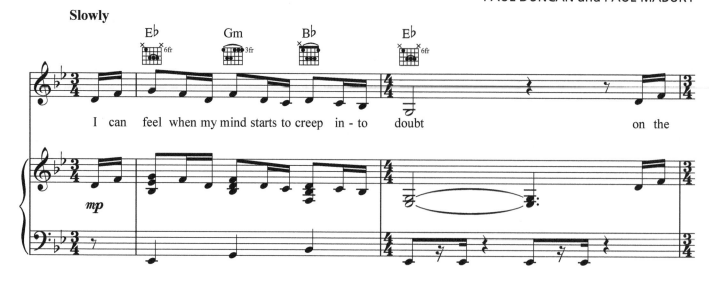

I can feel when my mind starts to creep in-to doubt on the

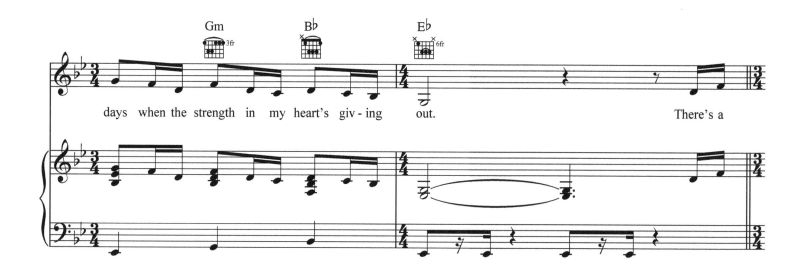

days when the strength in my heart's giv-ing out. There's a

light, but it hides from me deep in the cloud. There's a
prom-ise to play on re-peat in my head. When you